Letters to Jimbo

Letters to Jimbo

Poems by

Nancy Owen Nelson

Cover image by Donna Steele
Author photo by Nancy Owen Nelson

ISBN: 978-1-63980-855-7
Library of Congress Control Number: 2026934478

Kelsay Books
502 South 1040 East, A-119
American Fork, Utah 84003
Kelsaybooks.com

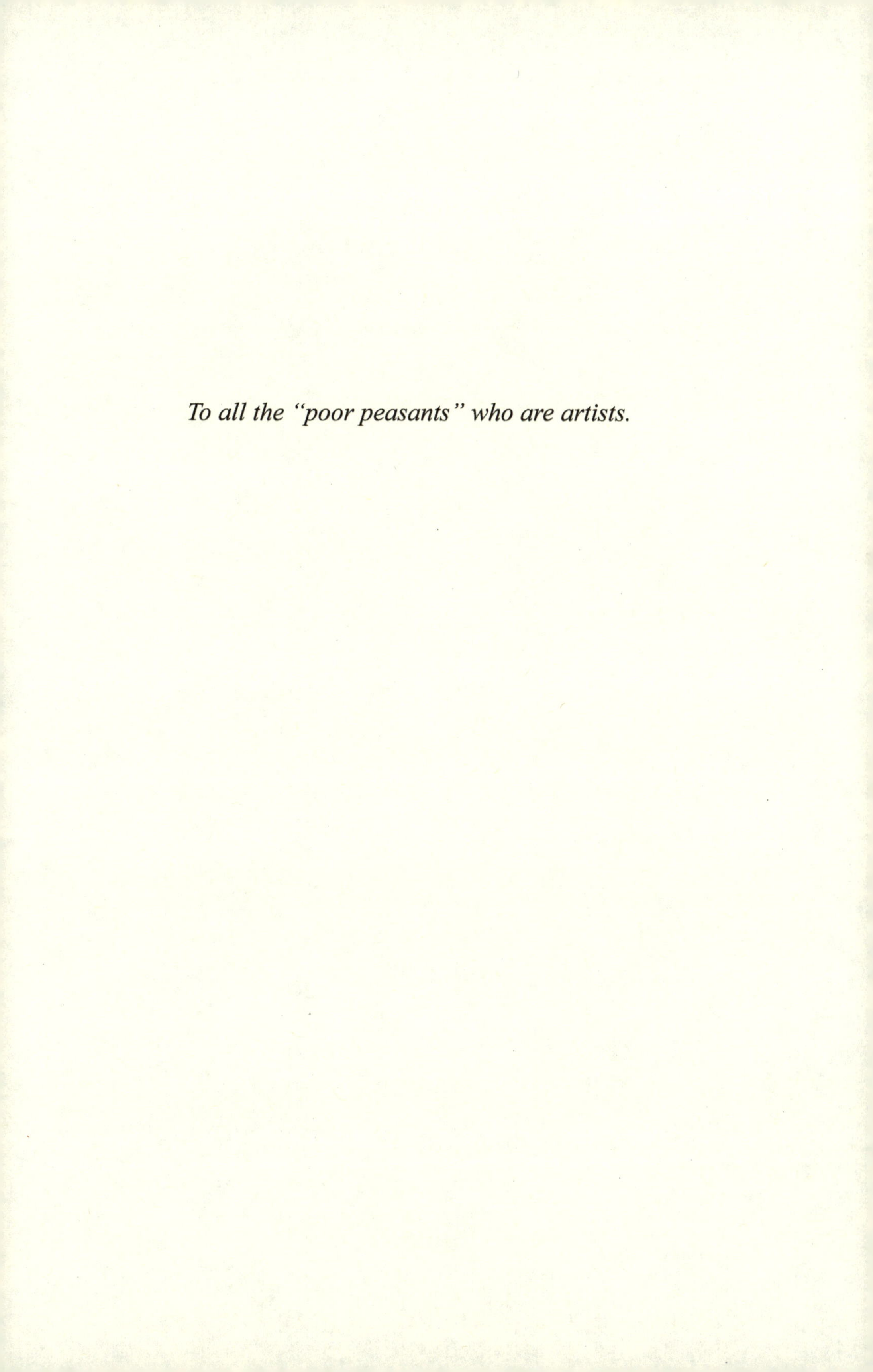

To all the "poor peasants" who are artists.

Acknowledgments

It is with deep gratitude that I share the story of *Letters to Jimbo.* My mentor Russ Thorburn continues his support of this recent effort. Friends have cheered me on in this endeavor when the way was not clear: writers and poets, Nancy Shattuck, Dawn McDuffie, Diane Decillis, Olga Klekner, Harry Moore, Hank Lazer, Jake Berry, Ken Miesel, and Donna Steele, whose lovely artwork graces the cover.

However, this book would not exist without Jimbo and his willingness to allow these poems to be made available for others. Note: I thank the editors of *Persimmon Tree* for publishing "The Afternoon You Danced in my Sunroom," Summer 2024, "Short Takes," persimmontree.org/summer-2024/pockets-of-joy/.

More Praise for *Letters to Jimbo*

The poems in *Letters to Jimbo,* reflecting the tentative, tender movements of a woman's heart from inured grief into an invitation for new intimacy after the age of seventy, are delicious in their ache, their Eros, their humility and their longing. With each poem, Nancy Owen Nelson adds new lines to love after seventy—a subject not often enough written about with such softened, sensualized, explorative candor.

The poems feel youthful, intense, secretive, excitable and uncertain, even born at the edge of an involuntary willingness to try again for intimacy. In the opening poem of the book, the narrator boldly inquires, "Handyman [Jimbo] are you the one who fixes broken hearts?" The steady self-disclosure in this evocative sequence of love poems never once falls into the banal.

Instead, the reader becomes invited into the emerging magnitude of what is actually at play—the unfreezing and the reopening of a heart to the liberation of desire, so that it might heal. Although the poet references love experience after seventy, what the reader experiences is the sensual, youthful, eternalized lushness of the falling in love with someone again: its colors, its tastes, its freedom, its febrile excitement after "an evening of touching."

And yet, perhaps the deepest delight in this collection is that the poems themselves—in how they emerge and how they are sequenced—seem to be paced and presented in the same careful, tentative, vulnerable and expressive way that both these depicted would-be lovers exhibit in their personal dance together, just as they themselves experience it.

—Ken Meisel, author, *The Light Most Glad of All*
and *Chasing Names on Nameless Water*

Excerpt from "Set-Back Days"

These letters, these poems, are my work, they
are my love labor, my gift to you, even when
sometimes they dive into murky, dark places,
like a miner descending into unknown blackness
of spirit. It is my hope that these gifts always
ascend into light and understanding.

Please remember this.

And thank you, Jimbo, for this work
you've given me.

Contents

Wanted: Handyman

You enter my side door. Your kneepads look as if
they're attached to your body. *Do you
ever take them off?* I will ask myself for weeks.

You arrive often, seems like every day,
backing your white van into my driveway,
instruct me on the facts of men and women,
differences I've talked about in academic papers
and classes, heard in lectures. *Women like little
pretty things, clutter,* you mumble, or perhaps
you say loud enough for me to respond, then
move into another room, claim I mumble,
not you. Claim I am a hoarder although
I've just lost my husband, moved 600 miles back
to a state where I'm not sure I'll find a place
to be or call home. Because I'm still grieving,
still touching his clothes—his shirts, robes,
can't let them go yet. Let go the stones that
are his body. Boxes of pictures of all the dead
still living in me. All this I cannot let go of.
Yet.

One day you'll say, *Your husband would want
you to be happy,* looking at me with eyes
that make me want to dive deep, seem to understand
who I am and what I've been through. You
always know, Handyman, beneath
the bravado, the rooster crowing about women
and men, about my clutter, about how you're
glad I'm *not in jail* when we haven't talked
for a day, somehow you always understand
my pain, my sadness, the depth of loss.

When I hear about the barbed wire, the camps
where your parents lived years of their young lives
under Nazi rule, I think I understand. You are
an old soul who carries their pain, and yours,
with you.

Soon I will learn that you spent years of sweat
and strain, your body aching with too much
labor, too little praise, love. Did anyone ever
hold you? Did anyone stroke your curly hair,
tell you you were beautiful, you were enough?
Did anyone, as have I, sniffed, whispered
into your ear like a rabbit, until your body
shook with delighted giggles?

You keep coming back. In between crafting
shelves and bookcases, repairing steps,
installing railings for my safety, you
instruct me on the proper way to drill
into drywall, placing your roughened
right hand over mine. *I don't mean
to be holding your hand,* you say.
You can hold my hand any time, I reply.
It comes out before I think about it.

Handyman, are you the one who *fixes
broken hearts,* whom women run to
for comfort, for relief? Was James
Taylor onto something?

Who are you, Handyman?

Play Sweet!

Get in the house, girl, you said
last week when I came out to see
you while you talked to my gardeners.
If I'd not known you these many months,
Jimbo, if I'd not talked with you for hours
about men and women, about our differing
ways of seeing the world, you, recently
released from commitment, I, released by
by a loved partner's death, I would have
condemned you to feminist hell, to torture
by females who had fought for their dignity
over centuries of abuse by men who spoke
this way to women.

I know you. I've seen the man who, beneath
the armor that keeps him safe from
a world in which he's had no say about who
he is, what he will do, carries in his breast
a tenderness, a *sacred* heart, not with thorns
or piercing sword, but one that strives to help
others, feels in every tender muscle the pain
of a young girl snatched and raped,
of the fighting in the Middle East, the turmoil,
division our country faces today.

Yes, I know you. Early on, you, who told me
you were glad I was *not in jail,* surprised
I had *more than one friend,* that I'm
a hoarder, while I fought back tears
as I tried to find a path through a dining room
cluttered, stacked, with random boxes,

in my new house, I despaired I'd ever
see the way through.

And then, when the tears stopped
(I don't think you knew I was crying),
you took in hand the chaos that was
my living room, my bedroom,
the notion of *feng shui* on your tongue.

What handyman knows about feng shui?
I muttered under my breath. But I let you
go, let you move and shape and look
at angles, asking *What do you think?*
Can we find something to fit this space?
until, for the first time, I saw a path
through the hell of my new jungle,
a possibility that this house, *my* new home,
could be a place of peace, of rest,
refuge.

That day in the yard, you said *I'm sorry.*
It touched my heart. Sometimes
when you visit, you say *I told myself*
I'd be nice. I call it *playing sweet,*
a phrase that in its southern-ness drips
not of honey, but of genuine, sweet
liquid of goodness.

And Jimbo,

I love you when you *play sweet.*

The Table

On a hotter-than-hell August
afternoon in North Florence, you sit
at your table—strewn with paper,
pen, stapler, folders, a plant given

by a friend for your new tiny house,
built from nothing, up from the gently
sloping hills of North Alabama,
an edge of Appalachian beauty.

You dreamed it. You built it. With hands
roughened by a life of labor, with body
still strong, but hearing the call of rest,
reflection. And now, you sit in cool

air, blessedly out of an oven
pressing against windows. On the table sits
a family photo—two parents, nine
children, you the toddler in your father's

arms, your blond-white curls slightly blow
in whatever breeze there was that day.
Today you will build a frame for yet
another family picture, this time

not one about love and hope, but about
barbed wire and hopelessness.
Circa 1939, Germany invades Poland.
An aunt caught in a net of Nazi terror.

Is it a concentration camp? Or a holding
camp? You do not know for sure.
But there, behind barbed wire, is Aunt Josefina,
her face defiant, proud, determined.

I am a woman, she says to you.
Is it sweat, or is it tears that run
Down your face? You are not sure.
You are certain of only one thing.

She will not submit.
Not now, or ever.

You Came for Me in the Cold, Wet, Night

First cool night of fall in Florence, October
bidding farewell to boiling heat, rainless
afternoons when, parched with thirst,
neighborhood grasses finally soak in moisture
An afternoon rain—just enough to give them hope.
You came for me when I wandered through the damp
dark streets of a village new to my eyes,
to my feet as I felt my way up an unfamiliar hill,
stumbled over protruding roots of an ancient
oak tree on the edge of a sidewalk with broken
concrete, stumbled toward the light of a friend's house.

Your voice was strained, tight, on the phone when
you asked where I was, where, not *why* I had left a room
where I felt invaded in my own home by the voice
of an old, trusted friend. *Call me when you want to come*
home, you said. And then, *I'm outside, I'll wait as long as you*
want me to. You only cared that I was safe, that you could
bring me back into a room where we have sat for so many
hours talking, holding hands, where you have massaged
my legs and I, yours, with strong hands honoring the feet
that have taken us through these many miles we've walked.

And in that room, you held me to your body a long time, held me
to you where I fit so well, my lips touching your neck, kissing it,
my frame fitting against yours in just the right places.

Such sweetness it was. You rocked us side to side, like two babies in a cradle. So gentle, and so caring. I spoke aloud. *Sometimes words don't matter.* And you agreed. with that low, familiar groan that comes from your chest when you hold and kiss me.

That those moments could last. That the torment, the confusion of daily life could be rendered quiet, could become simple, rocking motion of bodies rescued from a cold, wet night in fall, brought into warmth and healing.

Your Voice

It growls deep within your chest,
that rumble, like a contented cat,
when we talked for hours,
probed deep into the caves of the past
like miners who trust enough
to turn off their lighted helmets. I miss it.

This is one of those days, Jimbo,
like the ones, in the beginning,
when you were present, when I felt
the panic of so much built-up fear
from who knows what. I ran
faster and faster to get somewhere,
to restore life neatly into boxes—
goals, balance, health of mind and body,
obligations that my partner's passing
thrust upon me.
Then you would stop me, pull me close
to you. You'd say *breathe,* your voice
smooth and warm, a voice without irony.
Did I hear love in it? *Breathe one, two,*
three, four. Exhale. That's what they taught us
in the Navy. And always, always, Jimbo,
I was safe, safe inside the voice that
I imagine still resonates, still soothes my heart,
as if a gentle hand placed itself on my chest
with a blessing.

I long for it, long to be pressed against
you, to hear the deep yet gentle
growl, almost a purr that comes, I think,
from the place where your heart is buried deep.

Though buried still it is.

Consider the Artist

You built a tiny house from *ashes of the earth,*
you said, 700 square feet, wide windows
face south, peer into the street, a broad
porch for sitting, for grilling, for serving
friends who came to celebrate you,
you and your gift of constructing a home.
A place where, you said, you found peace
after a long day's work of body and mind,
exhausted from labor, from thinking
about your new life with all its hopeful
possibilities.

Today, the walls are bare where once they
held photos of loved ones, one framed
in barbed wire and bearing the pain
of family history, your daughters, an art piece
I gave you, painted by a friend. Cupboards
empty of cups that held the hot coffee
you offered me on a winter afternoon.
empty of plates we used when we
ate grilled tilapia, rice, salad,
(making sure, I did, that you had greens
to nurture your strong body, to ensure
it had strength to meet whatever
comes next). Empty of wine glasses,
thin stemmed, for red wine I tasted
while you sipped your screwdriver,
Tito's Vodka and orange juice every
night at 5 p.m. What a perfect name
for your drink of choice, *screwdriver,*
after all those years of handling tools
to create, to mend, to fix and make whole.

When I think of your creation, I think
of Stonehenge, those noble sarson
stones dragged thousands of miles
to a place where the ancients could
embrace nature's signs of changing
seasons. I want to see Stonehenge
someday, to feel the pulses of history,
of creation, of work that challenged
the body, the imagination. For me,
this tiny house is that—your art,
your self, your creation, a home.

This home with its simplicity, the care
of your touch, your mind's imaginings,
it is whole just as it is. But Jimbo, you
are gone from its walls, gone from
embrace of your art, embrace of a day
you'd return from labor to sit at your
table, contemplate your new path,
feel the pulses of family stories,
where of a night, you'd closed your eyes
early, a stuffed black and white
tiny cat next to your pillow. Where,
at least you told me so, you found
inner peace, your *high time.*

May you find your peace in this high
time.

May you come home.

Set-Back Days

We all have them, don't we, Jimbo?
I know you have yours. One day after
some incident upset you, you worked
in my garage, built shelving for the many
dusty tools I'd brought from Michigan,
drilled holes in the handles, organized
so that I could find what I needed.

That day, I think, it was cold, and I brought
you hot tea outside. I wanted you to be safe
and warm, not to suffer the dreaded rigors
that consume your body from time to time.
We hugged, and I felt the strain release in you.
Thank God you gave me work today,
you said. And it seemed to heal you,
patch up whatever cuts your heart suffered.

Today is a setback day for me, Jimbo. I write
my truths, and sometimes they hurt. They
risk, they challenge, they strive to understand.
These letters, these poems, are my work, they
are my love labor, my gift to you, even when
sometimes they dive into murky, dark places,
like a miner descending into unknown blackness
of spirit. It is my hope that these gifts always
ascend into light and understanding.

Please remember this.

And thank you, Jimbo, for this work
you've given me.

So Many Rooms

There were so many places to explore,
tantalizing, inviting, imagined talks
of your family history, explorations
into the many *rooms,* as you called them.
We could open doors for greater understanding.

We never entered most of those rooms,
never turned antique knobs like the one
on my front door, wrenching open,
then closing oh so carefully, pulling
shut until just the correct click, the catch of it.

We only tiptoed past the doors, whispering,
hoping (I was) that we'd enter, wander among
cluttered, half-filled boxes of confusion,
of mantras jammed, forced into truths
unraveled only with time, wander
together with patience, understanding—

Just as we unraveled our pasts, our differences,
what we shared—love of life, hope
for freedom for those unjustly yoked.
Surely, you said, *we will find that we are*
not as far apart as we seem.

We never entered those rooms. Never
pulled, turned the antique knobs rusted
into place by tradition, by willful blindness.

For this was only the beginning—abruptly
halted by fear, by *flight* over *fight,*
by necessity, without the comfort
of hands clasped in love and prayer.

Sweat

I weeded today, only a small plot in my front yard,
only a half hour in a late spring Alabama afternoon,
armed with a scuffle hand hoe, my face reddened by
effort. Only a half hour, yet sweat dripped down my neck,
my face flushed with effort. Last summer, to beat the heat,
early one morning I weeded raucous wild growth, hoped
to conquer the unconquerable. Anticipating your arrival
to discuss some handyman project, I showered,
lathered my body with *Beautiful* wash, scented
from special cologne, donned a sundress. I hardly
knew, hardly realized yet that I was doing it for you.
I scarcely sensed the stirrings in my belly, my chest,
when I knew you were on the way.

Sweat is good for you, you told me as we sat talking,
you opposite me in your work clothes.
It will clear out the pores. Healthy, cleansing.

And today, I pulled, then pushed the hand hoe
until, loosened from moist soil, those errant weeds,
roots upward in surrender, even in their uprooting gave
forth their earthy scent. And today, I cleaned out
the dead sprigs of a mum you planted last fall,
one I fretted would not live through my winter
angst, my neglect of watering.

But live it does, like the memory of my sweat,
my body slick with *Beauty* wash, anticipation,
a stirring in my chest.
My belly.
My heart.

The Afternoon You Danced in My Sunroom

It was midsummer, my first one back South, and I wondered
what the hell I was thinking? 99 degrees plus humidity
outside, but you in your work clothes and socks, your
forever knee pads, sunglasses looped over your T-shirt.
You were having fun, Neil Diamond's "Thank the Lord
for the Nighttime" on my Alexa. You sang as you gyrated,
twirled across the open room, an afternoon of freedom
from an old life. You spun, turned toward me and sang
along with Neil.

You danced away, then back, beckoned me to join as you
sang along, your day drenched with sweat and toil, duty.
Those few times we danced, when you pulled me to you
and away from my politics as I tried to speak to a senator,
or when you grabbed me at a Friday night jam session
of male musician friends.

On an evening, you let me lead the box step in the very sunroom
where you had your Arthur Murray debut. It was late winter.
This time, more focused, as if we might find a spot across the river
in Muscle Shoals, a club where we could pretend no one knew us,
where we could forget the day . . .

Jimbo, do you remember my laughter, my words, on the video?
Go Jimbo! This will make me happy when . . .

I didn't finish.
I think I meant

when
I look
at
this
film
later.

And
here
and
now,
tonight.
It
does
make
me
happy.
But
I
also
wait
for
the
next
dance.

Birthday/Earth Day

I.

I'm sad this morning. I haven't heard your voice
in a few days, *Hey there Miss Sunshine,* as it lightens.
lifts the air, in my cosmos. What I do hear are ghostly
talks we're *not* having on topics imprisoned
in many rooms we've never dared enter.

Politics or social issues come up. You are silent,
except for the faint grumble in your chest when
I try to put a different view on things. We do
not talk further.

Those forbidden topics lurk around me,
won't let me alone. As I separate paper and plastic
from garbage, I hear you say *I'll save the planet*
one more day with my cardboard cup I'm tossing
in the recycle bin. Your voice is ironic, and yet, when
we're together, you do toss the cup, cardboard,
paper, into what may seem to you a useless blue bin.

II.

As I read or listen to poetry on racial injustice,
as I hear a lecture on a book about freedom,
its many dimensions, interpretations, these topics
nag me. Yours can be a contrary voice, one that
seems to condemn. Do you mean it? You, the man
who has compassion for others' suffering?
These thoughts gather around me, muttering,
What would Jimbo say? Can he possibly believe
that his parents' story, their cruel sentence
as slaves in Nazi camps, is any less horrific than slaves
who inhabited our shores three hundred years
ago, even as early as my kin arrived? For me,
there is no question of the wrong done to
these two Polish youths, forced to labor
as slaves to an evil force. I have no doubt
that, as King stated, *Injustice anywhere*
is a threat to justice everywhere. Yes,
Jimbo. The horror your Stanley and Lucy suffered
stays with you, with your siblings, your
family, and now with me. Because I care
that they were treated like slave animals.
Because I care for you. Because they, like we.
are woven together in the fabric of humanity.
This is what I would say to you
if we ever had the conversation.

III.

In early days, you tell me
I need facts,
I need proof,
I want the truth.
And yet,
And yet,
you never say more, never offer
alternative ideas, a political meeting
I can attend that would support
race amity, social justice, health
of the planet, reform for prisons
in a state system that gloats over
incarceration of the sometimes innocent.
Never offer a church meeting that casts
me into hell because I believe in love,
upholds the absolute law of the Bible
as fact, unquestioned.

IV.

Your courageous parents prevailed,
arrived in Florence with two daughters,
in May 1949, probably at the Old Railroad
Bridge across the Tennessee River.
We visited it one morning, the sun glinting
off the river. I could hear pride in your voice.
They probably arrived right here, Stanley and Lucy,
with my two sisters, you said. Proud, yes,
Jimbo, of their courage, their grit, their desire
to make a life free from bondage to evil.

You and I do not talk about freedom,
but I do have the intoning of your
voice when we do speak,
caressing me with what feels
like love, leaving so much
unspoken.

And there's your birthday, April 20.
For that special day I give you
a favorite artist's rendering of the Old
Railroad Bridge. I hope you know
what it means to me. Like your tiny house,
this photo is you, is your family's struggle,
the simple strength you inherited from them.

And Jimbo,
do you know
your birthday
is two days before
Earth Day?

Sing!

You should sing! You've told me many times
as you worked on my house, drilling screws
into walls, hanging pictures, making sure they sat
evenly, balanced on the wall—such precision.
Such attention to detail. *You should sing*
with your musician friend. Ask him to let you
harmonize.

It felt familiar to me, that command to sing,
that desire that grows out of my bloodline,
my mother, her mother, and perhaps hers
before her . . . *Sing. It's a gift.*

I think back on voice lessons in college,
the teacher with white hair, limping
with a cane (a car accident somewhere
in Europe, I remember being told). She,
too said *Sing,* not with a caring voice,
like yours, but with an impatience,
perhaps with her own pain—the pain
of a body damaged by grinding metal,
by dissonance, discord.

Sing, she almost screamed, then the swift
raising of her hand grasped a cane,
crashed on the piano top (or so my
youthful, frightened self recalls)

until *Sing!* I could not. Too timid,
too fearful of failure. Perhaps too far
from the notion of any vocal gift
worth sharing.

Back then, I never finished that little song,
Frost's "The Pasture," gentle invitation to the reader,
the listener, to *come too,* when the songster goes out
to *clean the pasture spring,* to *rake the leaves away.*

And then you spoke up.
You should sing, you said.

So I sang again,
for me,
for you,
for that frightened young thing I was.

It was a solo at a local concert.
It was that little song about a pasture.

You were there, hidden near the back.
You came because you promised me you would.

And as I sang, I knew whatever lovely path
I would take, *whatever path,*

I wanted you to come along.

Sing "AMERICA"

I did not want to sing it, this so familiar song about
amber waves of grain and other mythologies
tied in with this nation, its genes soaked with power,
lust for territory.

Army kid as I am, I held these beliefs for decades,
watched my father march and salute, his pride in nation
apparent in his straight back, eyes peering forward,
his absolute service to something he loved.

I'd given it all up. Dad was dead many years when
I read about Vietnam, read the power and politics—
the Gulf of Tonkin Resolution, 1964. An attack
that never happened. A war that did not have to be.

Not to mention Iraq. Not to mention a false analogy
to 9/11, to people ruled by a tyrant, one in the sights
of another leader who wanted just to get even.

Not to mention lives that did not have to be lost.

Here I was, in the front row, surrounded
by altos and sopranos, singing a song I had recanted,
a concept rejected. A love of country unrequited,
a bitterness I thought would last my lifetime.

There you were, standing up among seated attendees,
at the back, far left. Your blond-white wavy hair shining.
Yes, you stood for the song, and my eyes moistened,
my throat caught. For just a moment I could not sing.

There you stood, behind you, your young parents
who survived enslavement until they found a way to live
beyond the barbed wire and within a safer, better place,
a life of dignity, work, family, survival.

And how I have wished we would *mend our*
every flaw. That we could be a country with
self-control. As I sang these words, I glanced
at the back of the room again.

You stood until the last note ended.

And I sang with full-throated joy.

Audio Text: After Silence

This day is golden, tiny breeze, North Alabama
summer holding back to let spring hover
just a few days more. Should be a day free
of gathering gloom, but the back of my brain
murmurs, will not let me rest. As I often do,
I think of you, Jimbo, with infant granddaughter
in your arms, holding, swaddling, watching
her sleep while you, man of labor, sit softly,
wrapping her in your love like a soft blanket.

Today, frantic voices do not stop, do not
let me rest, wondering. Are you finishing
a fence around your new house, or grading
your drive, or perhaps you are mowing, ready
to come to Florence tomorrow to mow again.
Perhaps you are talking to the bikers
who live close by, rough men you've
welcomed to gentleness with your ways.
Whatever you're doing, I should know
better than to worry. You will always build
community, despite your bluster, your teases,
your quasi-macho display necessary to who
you are.

Are you perhaps baking Amish muffins?
Muffins that I nibbled at 4 a.m. many a winter
morning, crumbs dropping onto bed clothes
while I snuggled beneath the warm blanket

you gifted me at Christmas. Both blanket
and muffins warmed me, kept the cold January
wind at bay outside my bedroom windows.

I will see you tomorrow, before the music
and the laughter, before my departure
to fetch a friend across the river.
Will you really come?

Then an audio text. Your voice emanates,
gentle and soft, reaches across the day's
hours of frantic thoughts, imaginings.

My heart is calm.

Under the Influence: Belly Buttons

Anesthesia will do wonders to loosen the tongue,
a vulnerable heart exposes itself freely.

You come to check on me Jimbo, a whole day
out of your busy life with grandkids, building
a fence, constructing a new home, a new life.

We talk easily today, solidity of friendship intact,
but mostly you make sure I'm comfortable
after robotic surgery, that I can stand and walk
safely. You watch me sleep, holding my hand
tightly as if to say *I'm here for you.* And when
I rise from my bed you hold me to you in the way
I love, our frames fitting together as they do.

Want to see my scars? I ask at one point. *Yes,*
you answer, curious about life as you always are.
I expose my belly carefully, just below one of five
exquisite wounds across my abdomen.

But alas, the belly protrudes, filled with air
from surgeon's method, but most troubling
are the wrinkles—baby, weight loss, age?
Why do I reveal this part of me to you Jimbo?
I lament, complain to you about age, furrows.
I want to show a perfect belly.

Show me yours, I demand, and there it is,
taut, flat, the belly of a working man. Beautiful.

What can I say? You've seen me now, imperfect,
a few years older, yet vital and vibrant as ever.
I long for words of comfort. They don't come,
but what comes is your kind, caring face,
the hand I hold again while I drift off to sleep.

I hear in the distance, like the kids we both were once,
Show me your belly button, and I'll show you mine.

Bound by the Word "Friend"

It all started at a poetry reading. That day
you sat next to me, alert, as if you had attended
poetry readings every day of your life. Indeed,
you were an interested listener. The poet
spoke of the 32 words for "love" in Eskimo,
so many that Innuits know exactly how
and whom they love.

I've not heard the end of that reading,
not when we speak of love.
To you I'm a "best friend" (or is that
someone else?), or, a higher level, perhaps
your "die-for friend." What exactly does
that mean? You would die for me, and I
for you? Does it mean being kept
forever in a bond of friendship, not
love, the deep passions of the body
and the mind, the spirit, the joining?

You parse my heart, and you parse yours, Jimbo.
Like I used to diagram sentences
in fifth grade English class, or like
I isolated and labeled frog eggs
in my college biology class, squinting
through the microscope, just so,
very grateful that I could see, identify,
that tiny life force of black spots.

Very grateful I would get class credit, very
grateful I could return to my textbooks
of English poetry, American literature,
home at last to territory I could navigate.

Jimbo, I don't know how to navigate this,
don't know how to lock up my feelings
in a steel cage that is my heart. I've read
that some species of frog eggs incubate at 2 degrees

for 25 days, hatch in 7 to 10 days
at 15 degrees. Will this love egg
that is my heart be freed to hatch?

And Jimbo, can you tolerate such cold?
Can I?

The New House

Last week I visited your new house,
so simply graced, so minimal, so like you—
spotlessly neat, not even dust
or grass on the floors. Minimal,
so like your goal to *simplify, simplify,*
as Thoreau tells is in *Walden.* You've labored
hours and months, days, in spring and summer.

This sweet little house is you—circular fence
around well-tended lawn, pin-neat kitchen,
bedrooms, walls graced with loved family photos,
your aunt behind barbed wire, two daughters—
little girls, young women—and the old bridge
photo, my gift to you for birthday, a bridge
that represents your parents' struggles
for freedom so many years ago.

Men lead lives of quiet desperation, writes Thoreau,
go to the grave with the song still in them.
Not you.
This little house you did not build with your hands
is now your place to be. A simple yard, a circular fence,
cattle gate closing the drive, and your signature guitars
built along the fence, *Sweet Home North Huntsville* carved
across one of them.

Clear path inside, uncluttered with vestiges
of life's business, unlike mine, where books
seem to reproduce and clutter, rearrange themselves
within a space that can hardly hold them, books

I may never read, but, by God, I'll shelve them
just in case.

Jimbo, you *are* a book. You've told me,
My book is my life, my walks, my talks.
my hammer, my soul. And I believe you.

It comforts me, as do our differences.
You have held the books I wrote
in your roughened hands, read them,
(I hope) loved them, though what I say
sometimes jolts you, lets you know me
a bit better.

Jimbo, I cannot wait to read your book.

Falling in Love After Seventy

Like it was yesterday, like it was North Alabama—
warm afternoons after class was out, red convertible
swaying back and forth over the river, cotton, soy
bean fields moving fast past us. Like it was prom,
except without the glittery dress with hooped skirt,
the gym decorations, not a football game, only excitement,
only anticipation at where we'd drive next—a small town,
a creek (I can't remember its name) where abandoned
WPA concrete construction sat idle,
quiet stream running past. Or a dam, another bridge
glinting in sunlight, its signs detailing the history of TVA.
Or excitement at the stories you would tell,
the past, yours and others, life you'd lived so very
different from mine, rooted in place and work, while mine,
a life of movement and constant change, of shifting place,
friends, schools.

Of shifting everything.

All this with the promise ahead of yogurt,
a generous cup of tart Vanilla Bean, topped with
a touch of chocolate, chopped Heath Bar pieces,
Reeses, or M&Ms of all colors, mixing deliciously,
relished by the bite. You often took a smaller portion,
perhaps thinking of your health, or remembering
habits you wanted to erase. But always the sweetness
of yogurt, or stories, of touches in my darkened hallway
at the end of the day.

Like remembering suddenly, with the touch of a hand
on mine, or on my back, or shoulder. that my body is
still alive, still pulsing with quivers of desire in the night
that left me fetal, clutching a bear I'd been given
years ago, for comfort after surgery. I call her "Thelly,"
named for two cats I'd owned with my beloved deceased.

I'm leaving her to you, Jimbo, so you won't forget me.

Like weeping through love songs we'd shared, like
rehearsing a tune I'd always wanted to sing,
as perfect as I'm able, recorded for you as a holiday gift.
As I practiced. I avoided the reality of the lyrics reminding me
how I feel, reminding me of the real possibility of your leaving,
of what I fear, that I would drift out to sea. That I would
go on, knowing my heart would break.

I can't allow those thoughts to stay with me,
can't allow the possibility that you would
really leave. Must not follow my own gripping
fear in the gut, that you, too, would disappear,
a figment of my distorted imagination.

And you did.
And then you reappeared.

Falling in love after seventy is lush, rich
in color, taste, touch. I fear. I do not want

to taste the bitter aftermath of leaving,
not like an afternoon of riding and stories,
of holding and talking, an evening of touching,
of possibility. Not at all like a dish of vanilla
yogurt topped with crushed Heath bar and M&Ms,
Reese's pieces, to balance vanilla's tartness.

Indeed, who are you, Handyman?

Notes

After the end of World War II, the United Nations Relief and Rehabilitation Administration was assigned to assist misplaced persons to resettle.

A farmer, John A. Locker, sponsored a number of such people to move to St. Florian, Alabama. Jimbo's parents were among those refugees who found a new life and the American Dream.

About the Author

Nancy Owen Nelson's poems appear in *The South Dakota Review, Graffiti Rag, What Wildness Is This: Women Write About the Southwest, The MacGuffin, This/That Lit* (online), and *Oberon.*

Her books include her memoirs, *Searching for Nannie B* (2015) and *Divine Aphasia: A Woman's Search for Her Father* (2021); her poetry chapbook, *My Heart Wears No Colors* (FutureCycle Press, 2018) and *Portals*: *A Memoir in Verse* (Kelsay Books, 2019); and her full-length collection *Five Points South*: *Poems from an Alabama Pilgrimage* (Kelsay Books, 2022), which was chosen as the 2022 Book of the Year by the Alabama State Poetry Society.

Nelson earned her B.A, in English and French at Birmingham Southern, and her Master's and Ph.D. degrees in English at Auburn University. She is the coordinator of the monthly Zoom program Poetry Vespers sponsored by the Unitarian Universalist Church of Detroit. She currently serves as Managing Editor of 7 Points Press in The Shoals, Alabama.

Most recently, Nelson has steered an effort to create a Poet Laureate for the City of Florence, Alabama.

www.ingramcontent.com/pod-product-compliance
Lightning Source LLC
LaVergne TN
LVHW051021080826
845145LV00009B/2729

* 9 7 8 1 6 3 9 8 0 8 5 5 7 *